IDAHU

TRAVEL GUIDE
2024

Discover the Beauty of Idaho

Donald M. Clark

All rights reserved. No part of this publication may be reproduced, distributed, or transmitted in any form or by any means, including photocopying, recording, or other electronic or mechanical methods, without the prior written permission of the publisher, except in the case of brief quotations embodied in critical reviews and certain other noncommercial uses permitted by copyright law.

Copyright ©Donald M. Clark, 2024.

Table Of Content

Chapter 1: Introduction to Idaho..................4
   History of Idaho........................4
   Geography and Climate..................9
   Culture and Traditions.................14
   Festivals & Events.....................25
   Local Cuisine..........................31

Chapter 2: Top Must See Attractions in Idaho......**38**
   Sawtooth Mountains.....................38
   Craters of the Moon National Monument..43
   Shoshone Falls.........................50
   Sun Valley Resort......................54
   Snake River Canyon.....................60

Chapter 3: Exploring Idaho's Heritage Sites......**66**
   Old Idaho State Penitentiary...........66
   Sacajawea Interpretive, Cultural, and Educational Center..........70
   Cataldo Mission........................75
   Minidoka National Historic Site........79

Chapter 4: Experiencing Idaho's Local Life......**84**
   Huckleberry picking in the Sawtooth National Forest. 84
   Explore Idaho's Artisan Beer Scene.....89
   Visit Idaho's Local Farmers Markets....95
   Native American Cultural Experiences in Idaho... 100

Chapter 5: Practical Information for Travelers in Idaho..................**106**

Accommodation Options in Idaho..........................106
Transportation in the State.......................................117
Shopping Tips and Recommendations...................129
Currency and Payment Methods..............................136
Chapter 6: Day Trips from Major Idaho Cities........143
Sawtooth Wilderness from Boise...........................143
Day Trip to Coeur d'Alene from Spokane.............150
Snake River Canyon from Twin Falls....................155
Silver City Ghost Town from Boise........................161
Chapter 7: Conclusion..167
Safety Tips for Tourists..167
Useful Phrases for Travelers..................................175

Chapter 1: Introduction to Idaho

History of Idaho

Idaho's history unfolds like a thrilling novel, with each chapter carved in the terrain and whispered by the wind. From the footsteps of ancient peoples to the pioneering spirit of settlers, this state has weaved a vivid tapestry across millennia.

Indigenous Inhabitants

Thousands of years ago, the territory now known as Idaho was home to a diverse group of indigenous cultures. The Shoshone people, with their strong respect for nature, left a legacy of petroglyphs engraved on canyon sides. These silent testaments provide an insight into their rich cultural practices and deep relationship with the earth. The Nez Perce, expert riders and ferocious protectors of their territory, also contributed significantly to Idaho's history. Their beautiful beadwork and handcrafted baskets are timeless representations of their artistic history.

Lewis & Clark

The Lewis and Clark Expedition arrived in the early nineteenth century, signalling a watershed moment. This historic moment chronicled the first recorded interaction between Europeans and Idaho's indigenous people. Standing at crucial spots such as Canoe Camp on the Clearwater River, one can practically hear the clink of canteens and the whispered whispers as they mapped a course through this unknown region. Their detailed writings provide invaluable insights into the different landscapes they visited, as well as their contacts with the people who live here.

The Gold Rush

During the great Western Gold Rush in the mid-1800s, there was an increase in the number of prospectors seeking their fortune. Idaho, with its abundant mineral riches, was no exception. Towns like Boise and Lewiston experienced a quick growth, with activity fueled by hopeful fortune seekers. Walking down these once-grand streets lined with old saloons, one can almost imagine the clamour of screams and clanging picks. While the gold rush finally faded, its legacy lives on in ghost towns and abandoned mining sites, concrete reminders of a time when hopes were brighter than gold.

Settlers and Homesteaders

Following the gold rush, a wave of settlers arrived, enticed by the promise of fertile agricultural land. These pioneers carved up homesteads in the untamed wilderness, braving severe winters and punishing terrain. Exploring antique farmsteads, one can practically feel the calloused hands clutching ploughs and the unyielding determination written on their cheeks. Their legacy lives on in the lovely communities that dot the region, a monument to their tenacity and pioneering spirit.

The Twentieth Century and Beyond

Idaho's industrialization began in the twentieth century. Hydroelectric power facilities came to existence, powering lumber mills and other industrial pursuits. Driving through enormous potato fields, one can not help but notice how important agriculture remains in moulding Idaho's economy. Today, Idaho is evolving, embracing modern developments while conserving its unique tradition.

A Journey through Time

Standing at the crossroads of history, gazing out over the vastness of Idaho, one feels a tremendous sense of timelessness. The whispers of the past blend with the present, producing a tapestry of stories of suffering, resilience, and cultural diversity. Listen for these echoes as you travel through Idaho. They act as a compelling guide, illuminating the heart and soul of this extraordinary state.

Geography and Climate

As you embark on your Idaho vacation, expect to be intrigued by a state with a surprisingly diversified geographical tapestry. Idaho's surroundings, from the towering peaks of the Rocky Mountains to the immense expanse of the Snake River Plain, guarantee an amazing experience. This tour looks into the state's distinctive geological formations and the ever-changing embrace of its climate.

A Realm of Towering Peaks

The gorgeous Rocky Mountains, which adorn the northern part of Idaho, are unquestionably the state's crown jewels. The Sawtooth National Recreation Area, called for its jagged peaks that resemble a huge saw blade, is a great example. Visitors are greeted by breathtaking views, crystal-clear alpine lakes, and a vast network of hiking and bike paths suitable for all skill levels.

Volcanic Wonders and Canyons of Enormous Size

Travelling south presents a drastic change in the terrain. The Snake River Plain, a massive volcanic plateau formed by prehistoric eruptions, covers a large chunk of Idaho. Craters of the Moon National Monument is located in this region, and it is a surreal wonderland of lava flows, cinder cones, and subterranean caves that demand exploration. Prepare to be transported to a landscape straight from a science fiction novel.

Furthermore, Idaho has Hells Canyon, the deepest river valley in North America, which runs along its western border. Imagine towering cliffs dropping hundreds of feet into the rushing

Snake River below, creating a spectacle that humbles visitors with the sheer strength of nature.

Desert Delights and Hidden Oases

Idaho's geographical variety goes far beyond mountains and valleys. Travelling southwest, you will come across the high desert, a mesmerising expanse of undulating sagebrush plains sprinkled with cacti and the occasional juniper tree. The stark beauty of this terrain exudes a peaceful calmness, while the huge open areas provide a sense of limitless freedom. Keep an eye out for hidden oases, such as those located along the Thousand Springs Scenic Byway, where crystal-clear springs emerge from the parched soil, nourishing pockets of colourful flora in the desert landscape.

A Symphony of Seasons

Idaho has a distinct four-season environment, with each giving its own particular appeal. Summers are hot and dry, especially in the desert regions. Sunscreen, a hat, and plenty of water are necessary companions for summer adventures. The mountains give welcome relief, with lower temperatures and the occasional refreshing afternoon thunderstorm.

Fall paints the state in a fiery display. Leaves turn vivid tones of red, orange, and yellow, especially in aspen forests at high elevations. Winter provides a blanket of snow, perfect for world-class skiing at renowned resorts such as Sun Valley. Be prepared for freezing weather during the winter months and pack appropriately. Spring offers a welcome warmth and the satisfaction of seeing a colourful explosion of wildflowers decorate the landscape. This season also corresponds with ideal whitewater rafting conditions on the Snake River, when snowmelt swells the rapids.

Navigating The Diverse Landscape

Given Idaho's incredible variation in terrain and temperature, preparing for your expedition necessitates a flexible strategy. Layering is crucial. Even in the summer, a light jacket might come in handy for cool mornings and evenings, while a waterproof shell is required for mountain exploration. Trails require sturdy hiking boots, and a swimsuit is a must if you intend to cool off in a pleasant lake or hot spring. Sun protection is essential year-round, so bring your hat and sunscreen.

Embrace the Unexpected

One last piece of advice: be prepared for the unexpected. Idaho's weather can change quickly, so staying updated about the forecast will help you pack correctly. Most importantly, accept the unexpected! Idaho's attractiveness stems primarily from its unique topography and climate. So go forth, explore with an open mind, and let the Gem State astound you with its alluring beauty.

Culture and Traditions

Idaho, known for its magnificent landscapes and outdoor adventures, also has a diverse and vibrant cultural tapestry. From the continuing history of Basque settlers to the deeply ingrained traditions of Native American tribes, the state provides a distinct blend of influences that will definitely enrich your vacation. This guide goes deep into Idaho's cultural environment, providing a road map for navigating the state's unique customs and traditions.

A Legacy of Basque Hospitality

Explore Idaho's rich Basque heritage and enter a world of warmth and vibrancy. Descendants of Basque sheepherders who arrived in the late nineteenth and early twentieth centuries have weaved their traditions into the state's fabric. Towns like Boise and Gardena proudly display the unique Lauburu (Basque flag) and host vibrant Jai Alai matches, a fast-paced handball game that demonstrates Basque agility. Immerse yourself in the rhythmic energy of a traditional , a drumming procession that lights up the streets. Do not pass up the opportunity to try a substantial shepherd's stew, a delectable tribute to Basque ranching tradition.

Echoes of Native American Culture

Idaho is home to a rich tapestry of Native American civilizations, including the Shoshone-Bannock, Nez Perce, and Coeur d'Alene tribes, who have lived here for millennia. Pay your respects at cultural institutions such as the Sacajawea Interpretive Center and the Coeur d'Alene Tribe Museum, where you can see the elaborate beadwork, powerful drumming traditions, and engaging storytelling that keep these civilizations alive. A powwow, a lively celebration of dance, music, and community spirit, provides a unique experience. Witness the colourful dress, ornate regalia, and unifying power of common ancestry.

A Year of Festivals and Celebrations

Idaho knows how to celebrate! Throughout the year, villages and cities come alive with colourful festivals celebrating everything from Basque culture to unique local traditions. Immerse yourself in the Boise Basque Festival, a springtime celebration of dance, food, and music that brings the Basque spirit to life. For those coming in September, the Huckleberry Festival in North Idaho provides a tantalising glimpse into the world of this exquisite berry. Enjoy huckleberry pies, ice cream, and a variety of other delights that honour this local gem. If you want a taste of the wild west, do not miss the exciting rodeos held in communities like Pocatello and Salmon.

Beyond The Surface

Idaho's cultural environment goes much beyond these noteworthy features. Explore the strong Hispanic heritage of places such as Caldwell, where the smells of sizzling fajitas and the sounds of lively mariachi music evoke Mexican influence. Explore German customs in communities like Dietrich, where you will find real German bakeries and a strong sense of community. Foodies will thrill at the Lewiston Lebanese Festival, which celebrates Middle Eastern cuisine with fragrant spices and exquisite delicacies. Art lovers may immerse themselves in the vibrant arts communities of Boise and Sun Valley, where local talent thrives in galleries, studios, and lively street fairs.

Experience Local Life

To have a genuinely immersed experience, go beyond the tourist sites and connect with the communities that make Idaho unique. Visit a local farmers market, a bustling hub where friendly vendors proudly display fresh food, homemade items, and locally produced honey. Strike up a discussion to learn about their lives, the seasonal rhythms, and the distinctive traditions passed down through generations.

Learn the Local Ropes

Learn the skill of fly-fishing, a practice that is strongly ingrained in Idaho's rivers and streams, to embrace your adventurous side. Stand shoulder to shoulder with professional instructors who will not only teach you how to cast a fly, but will also tell you about the local environment and the strong bond that Idahoans have with their waterways.

A Night Out With The Locals

Spend the evening at a neighbourhood bar, where the walls tell stories and the air is filled with pleasant banter. Listen to live music, ranging from bluegrass to blues, and enjoy the laid-back environment. You might even find yourself two-stepping with a friendly native, a truly authentic Idaho experience that avoids tourist traps and promotes true connection.

Respecting Traditions

As you discover Idaho's varied cultures and traditions, remember to be a gracious guest. When attending cultural events, dress modestly and be aware of any photographic limitations. Always obtain permission before photographing individuals, especially during religious occasions. Buy local craftsmen' items and learn a few basic greetings in the languages spoken here (Spanish and Basque are popular).

Festivals & Events

After delving into Idaho's cultural tapestry, let us take a look at some of the exciting festivals and events that keep these traditions alive. Here are a few highlights to consider while organising your trip:

Boise Basque Festival (April)

Immerse yourself in the heart of Basque culture at this colourful spring celebration. Enjoy traditional dance performances, wonderful Basque food, and the exciting sport of Jai Alai.

Huckleberry Festival (North Idaho, September)

Celebrate the legendary huckleberry, a tasty wild berry endemic to Idaho. Enjoy huckleberry delicacies in every possible form, from pies and ice cream to jams and drinks.

Lewiston Roundup (July)

Witness the thrilling action of a professional rodeo. This historic event includes bull riding, bronc riding, barrel racing, and other activities that highlight cowboys and cowgirls' abilities and daring.

Sacagawea Heritage Festival (August)

This event, held in Lemhi County, remembers the heritage of Sacagawea, a Shoshone woman who played an important role in the Lewis and Clark expedition. Enjoy cultural demonstrations, historical reenactments, and traditional Native American cuisine.

Sandpoint Festival on Lake Pend Oreille (August)

Immerse yourself in the grandeur of the arts at this prestigious music festival. Renowned musicians from across the country adorn the stage, delivering a wide range of musical styles to suit every taste.

Local Cuisine

Idaho's culinary scene reflects its many cultural influences. Here are some foods you must try:

Basque

Enjoy a substantial shepherd's stew, a glass of Rioja wine, and luscious Basque cheesecake.

Native American

Try frybread, a wonderful fried dough that is commonly paired with savoury toppings such as stews or veggies. Do not miss out on trying huckleberry dishes, which are distinctive to Idaho.

American West

Enjoy a delicious steak or succulent ribs at a local grill. For a truly cowboy experience, try some beef jerky, a tasty dried meat snack.

International Influences

Discover the rich Hispanic and Middle Eastern communities' delectable dishes. Enjoy sizzling fajitas, fragrant Lebanese mezze platters, and other delicious delicacies.

Remember, this is only a sample of the many gastronomic experiences available in Idaho. Be sure to look beyond these choices and discover the distinct cuisines available at local restaurants, cafes, and farmers markets.

Festivals & Events

Idaho's magnificent scenery and outdoor experiences are obviously appealing, but the true heart of the state pulses through its vibrant festivals and events. Throughout the year, communities come alive with events that highlight Idaho's diverse cultural and traditional heritage. This book invites you to take a festive journey via iconic events and hidden jewels that will enhance your exploration of the Gem State.

Springtime Celebrations

Spring fills Idaho with brilliant wildflowers, and the celebratory mood blooms. The Boise Basque

Festival takes place in April in the capital city of Boise. Immerse yourself in the lively sounds of the txistu (a traditional Basque flute) and the rhythmic stomping of the Eskeulari dancers in their vibrant costumes. Enjoy the tantalising aromas of sizzling chorizo and steamy bowls of garlicky lamb stew emanating from food vendors. Witness the fast-paced sport of Jai Alai, in which participants propel a ball against a wall in an impressive display of agility.

Summertime Delights

Summer is filled with a plethora of festivals catering to a variety of interests. For a taste of the Wild West, attend the Lewiston Roundup in July. The air crackles with excitement as cowboys and cowgirls demonstrate their grit and talent in bronc riding, bull riding, and barrel racing, resulting in a memorable display.

For art lovers, the Sandpoint Festival in Lake Pend Oreille in August is a captivating event. Nestled on the scenic lakeshore, this renowned music festival provides a varied spectrum of musical styles, from heartfelt blues and jazz to thrilling indie rock and classical music. In between shows, visit art exhibits showcasing local and regional talent, or indulge in scrumptious culinary offerings from a variety of vendors.

Fall Festivals

As autumn colours the landscape in gold hues, Idaho hosts one-of-a-kind festivals celebrating the harvest's wealth and rich cultural legacy. In September, travel north to attend the Huckleberry Festival. This eccentric event honours the iconic huckleberry, a delightful wild berry endemic to Idaho. Towns convert into huckleberry paradises, with merchants selling huckleberry pies, ice cream, jams, syrups, and even craft brews flavoured with this distinct flavour. Immerse yourself in the celebratory environment with live music, cooking demos, and family-friendly activities honouring this delicious little fruit.

Honouring Heritage

Idaho has a diverse tapestry of Native American cultures, and their rituals are attractively shown throughout the year. The Sacajawea Heritage Festival, held in Lemhi County in August, honours Sacagawea, a Shoshone woman who played an important role in the Lewis and Clark expedition. Travel back in time with historical reenactments that bring the expedition's trip to life. Experience cultural demonstrations that highlight the beauty and expertise of the Shoshone-Bannock tribes, such as elaborate beadwork, traditional music and dance performances, and storytelling sessions that weave tales passed down through generations.

Beyond the Big Names

Idaho's festival culture is charming not only because of the big events, but also because of the smaller, more unique gatherings that reflect the character of individual villages. In June, visit Wallace for the Silver City Days, a lively celebration of the town's rich mining history. Expect parades, live music, historical reenactments, and even a funny "Gold Panning Olympics." In October, do not miss the Peculiar Pumpkin Patch Festival in Grangeville, which offers a taste of small-town charm. This unique event honours the simple pumpkin with contests, live music, pumpkin carving demonstrations, and even a "pumpkin catapult competition" that will make you smile.

Essential Tips for Festival Fun

To optimise your festival experience in Idaho, consider these helpful tips:

Dress for the Weather

Idaho's weather can be variable. Pack clothes and be ready for sun, rain, or even a chilly breeze, depending on the season and location of the festival.

Sunscreen and Hat

Many festivals take place outside, so make sure to bring sunscreen.

Carry Cash

While most vendors take credit cards, certain smaller festivals may require cash payments.

Arrive Early to Popular Events

Parking at major festivals can fill up quickly, so arrive early to get a decent location.

Idaho's diverse and vibrant festivals provide more than simply magnificent landscape. Embrace the holiday spirit, immerse yourself in the rich cultural tapestry, and make memorable memories as you travel across the Gem State.

Local Cuisine

Idaho, known for its magnificent landscapes and outdoor activities, also has a surprisingly broad and thriving culinary culture. This book delves into the core of Idaho's gastronomic offerings, bringing you on a delectable journey that goes beyond traditional tourist cuisine.

Basque Bounty

Indulge in a warm hug at a traditional Basque restaurant. The air is filled with the smells of garlic and cooking stews, and the energetic chatter creates an inviting mood. The shepherd's stew, a hearty, comforting dish traditionally made with slow-cooked lamb or mutton, delicate veggies, and chunky beans, takes centre stage here. Each spoonful contains a symphony of delicious aromas, well balanced by the meat's earthy undertones and the broth's richness. No Basque feast is complete without a glass of Rioja wine, a strong Spanish red that cuts through the stew's richness and perfectly complements its tastes. And finally, what? The Basque cheesecake is a revelation: it is rich, creamy, and topped with a hint of caramelised sugar. Indulge in this homage to the simple yet magical power of quality ingredients.

Bite of the Wild West

Idaho's ranching legacy extends beyond broad plains and breathtaking mountains to include hearty and tasty cuisine. Treat yourself to a steak from a local grill. The meat is of outstanding quality, perfectly cooked and full of flavour. For a genuinely authentic experience, try beef jerky. This tasty, dried pork nibble is a cowboy favourite and the ideal pick-me-up to fuel your adventures. Imagine the sun setting over a large canyon, a salty breeze blowing across your hair, and a gratifying chew of jerky - pure Idaho enchantment.

Native American Flavors

Take a culinary journey that celebrates the amazing traditions of Idaho's Native American tribes. Explore the delectable world of frybread, a versatile fried dough that can be used to express one's creativity. Serve it with delicious stews, fresh veggies, or even salsa. Each mouthful provides a pleasant contrast between the crunchy surface and the fluffy interior. Discover the distinct flavour characteristic of huckleberries, a wild berry cherished by Native American tribes for years. From fluffy pancakes brimming with juicy huckleberries to delicious jams and jellies, these versatile berries provide a taste of Idaho summertime.

The World on a Plate

Idaho's culinary culture is not limited to local delicacies. The state has benefited from the culinary traditions of vibrant Hispanic and Middle Eastern communities. Immerse yourself in the vibrant atmosphere of a Mexican restaurant, where the aroma of cooking fajitas fills the air. These Tex-Mex favourites, which include marinated slices of beef or chicken served on warm tortillas with all of the trimmings, are a sensory delight. A mezze plate allows you to immerse yourself in Lebanese cuisine. This symphony of tiny plates is bursting with hummus, baba ganoush, falafel, and tabbouleh, providing an explosion of flavour and texture in every bite.

Experience the Soul of Idaho's Cuisine
Idaho's gastronomic experience goes well beyond eateries. Visit a local farmers market, a thriving place where passionate farmers and craftspeople showcase their produce. Here, you

can walk among rows of freshly harvested veggies, lush berries, and fragrant herbs, getting to meet the people behind the food. Chat with vendors, learn about their practices, and purchase fresh, seasonal ingredients to prepare your own Idaho feast.

Embrace the Spirit

For a more immersive experience, try taking a cooking lesson at a ranch or farm. Learn the secrets of classic cuisine from knowledgeable locals. Imagine yourself making fried bread dough, learning the skill of slow-cooking a Basque stew, or preparing the ideal steak on a cast-iron grill. These encounters not only increase your taste for Idaho food, but also provide you with unforgettable memories to take home.

By exploring Idaho's rich gastronomic landscape, you will realise that the state has more to offer than magnificent beauty. From the soothing warmth of Basque cuisine to the distinct flavours of Native American customs, your taste senses will be taken on a journey as memorable as the state's natural splendour.

Chapter 2: Top Must See Attractions in Idaho

Sawtooth Mountains

The Sawtooth Mountains, a crown jewel of Idaho's wilderness, entice adventurers with their stunning peaks, pristine lakes, and bright wildflower fields. As a seasoned hiker, I can certainly state that they provide an unrivalled experience for outdoor enthusiasts of all levels.

A Journey through many Landscapes
Your journey through the Sawtooths begins at the trailhead, when the crisp mountain air awakens your senses. Sunlight streams through the deep evergreen forest, creating a dappled mosaic on the woodland floor. The earthy aroma

of pine combines with the beautiful chattering of birds, resulting in a natural symphony. As you ascend, the landscape changes. Rugged switchbacks test your endurance, but the payoff is clear. When you reach a high point, the world unfolds in a breathtaking vista. Emerald lakes sparkle like scattered gems, reflecting the snow-capped hills that penetrate the blue sky. The huge Sawtooth National Recreation Area extends as far as the eye can see, a tapestry of craggy mountains, verdant woods, and dazzling lakes. A sense of amazement sweeps over you, as you form a deep connection with nature's wild beauty.

Beyond The Grand Vistas

The Sawtooths provide more than just beautiful views. Each step along the walk exposes a hidden gem: a flowing waterfall pouring over moss-covered rocks, a clearing bursting with vivid wildflowers in a riot of colours, or a gorgeous bald eagle soaring effortlessly overhead. Perhaps you will see a lively marmot scurrying across the rocks alongside a crystal-clear lake, or be serenaded by the cascading power of a secret waterfall. Sharing a campfire with fellow hikers under a canopy of stars, exchanging stories and forming new connections, generates lifelong memories.

Tailoring Your Adventure

The Sawtooths offer a diverse range of hiking opportunities. A path awaits exploration, ranging from simple lakeside strolls to strenuous multi-day backpacking trips. Novice hikers might pick picturesque pathways such as the Redfish Lake Loop, which provide stunning vistas without requiring arduous climbs.

Experienced hikers may choose the famed Sawtooth Traverse, a multi-day expedition through the centre of the mountain range. For a taste of history, the large Hotel Trail leads to the remnants of a large lodge, which provide an insight into the region's past.

Important Tips for Your Sawtooth Journey

To ensure a safe and fun exploration, consider these useful tips:

Planning is Paramount
Carefully research trials and choose one that is appropriate for your expertise and fitness level. Popular trails include the Redfish Lake Loop, Sawtooth Traverse, and Grand Hotel Trail.

Embrace the Elements

Mountain weather is typically unpredictable. Pack layers of clothing for changing temperatures, rain gear for unexpected downpours, sunscreen, and a wide-brimmed hat for protection.

Respectful Exploration

The Leave No Trace principles are vital. To maintain the fragile environment, pack out all rubbish, limit the impact of campfires, and stick to approved pathways.

Embrace the Local Charm

Charming communities such as Stanley and Redfish Lake provide a sense of Idaho's mountain culture. Enjoy a delicious lunch at a local lodge, browse through unusual gift shops, or simply unwind and absorb up the laid-back vibe.

Hiking in the Sawtooth Mountains is an incredible experience that goes beyond simply physical endurance. It is about challenging yourself, discovering the great beauty of nature, and making lifelong experiences. So, lace up your boots, pack your backpack, and prepare to be swept away by the Sawtooth Mountains' grandeur. They await with wide arms and breathtaking splendour.

Craters of the Moon National Monument

Standing on the precipice of the Kings Bowl overlook in the Craters of the Moon National Monument, a stunning view unfolds. Volcanic cinders crunch beneath your boots, and the wind whispers secrets through the sturdy sagebrush. A stark patchwork of black lava flows, carved cones, and seemingly endless craters spreads beyond the horizon, creating an otherworldly landscape strikingly similar to the moon's barren beauty. Embark on a geological journey through this amazing monument, where volcanic fury has carved a country unlike any other.

A Fiery Past

Step back in time from 15,000 to 2,000 years ago as you explore the intriguing geological story revealed at the visitors centre. Interactive exhibits and informative displays provide a clear depiction of the massive volcanic explosions that created this amazing terrain. Molten lava spilled across the area, forming the stunning black features that dominate the contemporary landscape. Gain a better understanding of the raw strength that created this magnificent edifice.

A Self-guided Tour Through Time

Take a self-guided driving tour along the picturesque circle road that runs through the centre of the monument. Every turn reveals breathtaking landscapes, providing a glimpse into the heart of a volcanic wonderland. Stop at the aptly called Kings Bowl viewpoint to marvel at the sheer size of this huge hole. Nearly a mile wide, its cratered floor, studded with smaller cinder cones, transports the mind back to the volcanic mayhem that created this bizarre environment.

Short interpretative paths encourage additional investigation. Hike the Spatter Cones Trail to see these intriguing chimney-like formations created when molten lava splattered and solidified in mid-air. Each creation demonstrates the raw power of volcanic forces.

Delving Deeper

The Cave Loop Trail offers a very unique experience by taking you into the subterranean environment. Descend into a cold, wet lava tunnel, where sunlight filters through a hole in the roof to cast an ethereal glow on the cavern walls. Intricate lava structures and remnants of old ice flows tell stories of a bygone past. The only sounds are the drip-drip of water and the crunch of your boots, making this a genuinely awe-inspiring journey.

Beyond The Black

While the volcanic scenery takes centre stage, the Craters of the Moon National Monument is also home to a diverse range of life that has adapted to the harsh environment. Sharp-eyed visitors may notice robust sagebrush, with its silvery-green leaf hanging tenaciously to life. Wildflowers bloom in defiance of fissures in the lava rock, demonstrating nature's undying vigour. Keep your ears open for the beautiful calls of songbirds such as the Brewer's sparrow and the western meadowlark, which seek sanctuary in the scattered islands of greenery. A chance glance might reveal a jackrabbit or a coyote dashing across the plains, a reminder that life can thrive even in the most unlikely locations.

Plan Your Lunar Exploration

To make the most of your visit to the Craters of the Moon National Monument, consider these helpful tips:

Be Weather-Wise

Temperatures can vary greatly throughout the day. Pack layers of clothing and do not forget sunscreen, especially during the heat. Remember that shade is uncommon on lava flows.

Hydration is Key

Bring plenty of water to remain hydrated in the arid desert.

Sturdy Footwear is Essential

Uneven terrain needs appropriate footwear with strong traction.

Embrace the Silence

Leave your music devices behind and immerse yourself in the natural environment.

Tread Lightly

Stay on approved routes to maintain the delicate environment and preserve the distinctive geological characteristics for future generations.

Stargazing Paradise

With minimal light pollution, the Moon's Craters provide great astronomy possibilities. Bring a star chart or use a stargazing app to identify constellations and other cosmic delights.

The Craters of the Moon National Monument will leave a lasting impression. It is a journey back in time, a glimpse into the raw power of the Earth, and a tribute to life's eternal essence. So pack your spirit of adventure and prepare to be transported to another universe, right here on Earth.

Shoshone Falls

Nature's raw strength rarely disappoints, as Shoshone Falls, Idaho's "Niagara of the West," demonstrates. The Snake River, a critical artery that runs through the state, experiences a drastic alteration. As I stood on the brink of the Snake River Canyon, the wind blasted through my hair, causing a fine mist to dance on my skin. The huge river churned and raged below, ending in a stunning plunge over a horseshoe-shaped rock.

Shoshone Falls stands 212 feet tall, approximately 45 feet higher than its better known relative. However, the sheer volume of pouring water steals the show. Snowmelt and other tributaries feed the Snake River, transforming it into a raging torrent as it approaches the cliff. The ensuing spectacle is a breathtaking symphony of strength and beauty. The churning water produces a continual mist, creating rainbows that appear as ghostly apparitions against the canyon walls.

The trek to Shoshone Falls starts with a lovely drive down the Snake River. The dry terrain, speckled with sagebrush and juniper trees, opens before the visitor's gaze. The roar grows louder as you approach the falls, serving as a continual reminder of the strength that lies ahead. There is plenty of parking, and a well-maintained route goes to the canyon's rim, where you can enjoy a beautiful view.

However, the viewing platform is only the beginning. A walk down the Lower Promenade is strongly suggested for fully appreciating the falls' magnificence. Here, you will be closer to the churning water, feeling the full force of the cascading torrent. The spray provides a cool contrast to the afternoon sun, and the noise, while tremendous, has a strangely relaxing effect. It is a natural symphony, a basic energy that inspires meditation and awe.

Shoshone Falls is more than just a beautiful sight; it is also a historically significant location. The Shoshone-Bannock tribes have lived on these grounds for millennia, and the falls retain unique significance in their culture. According to legend, a young Shoshone woman went over the falls in a desperate act of defiance to avoid an undesirable marriage.

Beyond its beautiful and historical value, Shoshone Falls Park provides a range of activities for people of all ages. The informative interpretive centre teaches visitors about the canyon's geology and the falls' ecological relevance. Families can enjoy well-kept picnic spots, playgrounds, and a concession stand. Adventurers can take a boat excursion that offers a unique perspective on the falls from below.

As the sun sinks below the horizon, throwing an orange glow across the canyon walls, it is time to consider leaving. However, a persistent longing persists: to see the metamorphosis of the falls under the shroud of a starry night. You will leave Shoshone Falls with a sense of amazement and a deeper appreciation for nature's strength and beauty. It is a powerful reminder that the most breathtaking sights are not found in bustling cities or man-made wonders, but in nature's raw, untamed beauty.

Sun Valley Resort

Sun Valley, set amidst Idaho's majestic Sawtooth Mountains, has long attracted skiers, celebrities, and outdoor enthusiasts alike. This renowned resort town flawlessly combines opulent lodgings and world-class services with unrivalled access to pristine slopes and magnificent scenery. Guests will have a memorable vacation experience here, surrounded by a rich history and timeless charm.

A Legacy of Skiing Excellence
Sun Valley's story is inextricably tied with the sport of skiing. In the 1930s, visionary businessman Averell Harriman envisioned a winter wonderland to rival Europe's prestigious resorts. His idea became a reality with the construction of Sun Valley Lodge, a huge stone

edifice that exudes beauty and warmth even today. The historic lobby, with its distinctive red chairs dangling from the ceiling as a symbol of Sun Valley, brings guests back to the golden age of skiing. Renowned Hollywood icons such as Clark Gable and Gary Cooper have already frequented these halls, adding to the resort's rich heritage.

Hitting the Slopes

Sun Valley has two different mountains that accommodate skiers of all skill levels. Bald Mountain, commonly known as "Baldy" by locals, is a playground for experienced skiers. Thrilling black diamond runs like "War Eagle" and "Christmas Bowl" test even the most advanced skiers while providing beautiful views of the surrounding valley. Intermediate skiers will find a wealth of blue slopes winding through the stunning scenery, allowing unlimited opportunities to perfect technique and experience the exciting freedom of carving turns. Expert skiers can go beyond the bounds into the famed "Baldy Bowls" for an unforgettable backcountry adventure, always escorted by a qualified guide for safety.

Dollar Mountain, on the other hand, is ideal for beginners and families. Gentle slopes and designated learning areas provide the ideal setting for taking your first cautious steps on skis or enrolling your children in professional ski lessons. Seeing a child's face light up with delight and accomplishment after their first successful run down Dollar Mountain is a genuinely rewarding experience that they will remember for years.

Beyond The Slopes

Sun Valley's enchantment lasts far beyond the winter months. As the snow melts, a colourful summer season begins, with a range of activities to suit every interest. Hike along miles of picturesque pathways lined with wildflowers, which lead to cascading waterfalls and breathtaking views. Take a picturesque gondola ride to the summit of Baldy for breathtaking views of the valley. Golfers can put their skills to the test on championship courses developed by legends such as Robert Trent Jones Jr., while fly fishermen can cast their lines in the Big Wood River's beautiful waters.

Unwinding with Style

Following a day of action, guests can relax at Sun Valley's world-class spas. Soothe hurting muscles with a deep-tissue massage, renew your skin with a personalised facial, or simply relax in the tranquil spa environment. The resort also has a selection of pools and hot tubs, great for soaking in the warm Idaho sunshine and letting your cares melt away.

A Culinary Adventure Awaits

Sun Valley's restaurant options range from informal pub fare to upmarket fine dining, catering to even the most discerning palates. Enjoy a delicious lunch at the historic Sun Valley Lodge, where outstanding chefs produce delectable meals accompanied by beautiful panoramic vistas. For a more relaxed ambiance, go through the lovely village and discover hidden gems selling anything from homemade pizzas to superb steaks.

Exploring Ketchum's Charm

Sun Valley integrates smoothly into the picturesque town of Ketchum, providing depth to the overall experience. Stroll down the colourful Main Street, which is lined with art galleries, unusual stores, and cosy cafes that emanate a friendly mountain town atmosphere. Browse through locally manufactured goods, have a scoop of huckleberry ice cream (a unique Idahoan specialty), or simply people-watch and soak up the relaxed environment.

Sun Valley

Sun Valley is more than just a resort; it is an experience. It is the incredible adrenaline rush of slicing down a perfect slope, the tranquillity of a calm trek through a wildflower meadow, and the warmth of making lifelong memories with loved ones. It is a destination where luxury meets adventure, where history is whispered through majestic buildings, and where the mountains' magic lasts. So pack your bags, embrace your adventurous spirit, and get ready to be enchanted by Sun Valley's ageless enchantment.

Snake River Canyon

The Snake River Canyon, a massive gorge carved into the earth's surface, is more than just a picturesque beauty; it is a tribute to nature's unstoppable strength. It stretches over 1,000 miles along the Idaho-Oregon border and has depths of more than 6,000 feet, making it one of North America's deepest canyons. Standing on the rim, one is humbled by the sheer scale of this natural marvel.

A Tapestry of Colors and Texture

The canyon walls, sculpted by millennia of erosion, form a captivating canvas of brilliant colours. Fiery oranges, deep reds, and charcoal blacks blend to form a fascinating geological masterpiece. This multicoloured display is enhanced by the ever-changing light, which casts new light on the canyon walls with each passing hour.

Exploring Different Locations

The Snake River Canyon can be explored from a variety of access sites located strategically throughout Idaho and Oregon. Each site provides a distinct perspective and experience.

Hell's Gate State Park

This park offers stunning vistas and a breathtaking view of the canyon's grandeur. Informative displays illuminate the canyon's geological history and the distinct environment it sustains.

Thousand Springs Scenic Byway

This picturesque trail follows the canyon rim, providing a steady view of the Snake River flowing through the depths below. There are numerous pull-offs where you can pause and take in the canyon's magnificence.

Consider whitewater rafting activities, which are accessible in some areas of the river, for an even more thrilling experience. These thrilling trips provide a close-up look at the force of the Snake River as you traverse its rapids while flanked by towering canyon walls.

Encountering Wildlife

The Snake River Canyon is more than just a natural wonder; it also serves as a sanctuary for a variety of wildlife. Soaring across the pure blue sky, you could notice a gorgeous bald eagle, its white head a stark contrast to the azure expanse. Bighorn sheep, masters of agility, cross the almost difficult terrain on the canyon walls, while the haunting call of a coyote in the background reminds us of the untamed wilderness that still exists here.

Plan Your Visit

To make the most of your visit to the Snake River Canyon, consider these helpful tips:

Choosing Your Access Point

Research the numerous entry points in Idaho and Oregon to choose the one that best suits your needs.

Being Prepared

The weather in the canyon can be unpredictable. Pack layers of clothing, sunscreen, a hat, and durable shoes. Wind can be strong, so keep any loose belongings fastened.

Respecting the Environment

The Snake River Canyon is a sensitive ecology. Stay on approved trails, take out all rubbish, and leave no trace.

Embrace the Adventure

The canyon offers a limitless variety of activities, from picturesque walks and whitewater rafting to simply finding a peaceful area to soak in the breathtaking scenery. Whatever way you choose to experience it, the

Snake River Canyon will definitely leave an indelible impression on you.

Chapter 3: Exploring Idaho's Heritage Sites

Old Idaho State Penitentiary

The Old Idaho State Penitentiary's enormous iron gates creak open, revealing a stark courtyard illuminated by the chilly light of a northern exposure. Towering grey stone walls, aged and engraved by time, rise on all sides, casting a gloomy atmosphere over the grounds. History is more than just on exhibit here; it hangs heavy in the air, speaking of misery and defiance.

Stepping inside the threshold, one is immediately struck by the weight of history. The silence is heavy, interrupted only by the creak of floorboards underfoot. It is a quiet filled with untold stories of pain and resilience that reverberate within the walls themselves.

The cell blocks, each a grim reminder of a bygone period, are in stark contrast. These restricted quarters were narrow and utilitarian, providing little comfort to their occupants. The limited accommodations for those confined here included a single cot, a thin blanket, and a single barred window that provided a tempting view of freedom that was forever out of reach. Rough brick walls bore witness to the passage of time, with faded graffiti serving as a harsh reminder of desperate appeals for connection and a life left behind.

The solitary confinement cells, possibly the most frightening part of the jail, provide a sense of complete isolation. Imagine being imprisoned away in near-complete darkness, cut off from human contact, with just the flicker of a single bare bulb puncturing the interminable hours. This unsettling reminder of the psychological toll of prolonged captivity contrasts sharply with the grandeur of the warden's office.

With its towering ceilings and ornately carved furniture, the warden's office evokes a life of power and control. Decisions were made, fates were sealed, and the daily operations of this harsh institution were monitored. The juxtaposition of these locations emphasises the sharp distinction between those wielding authority and those who were subjugated to it.

But the story is not just about sadness. The penitentiary's library, a haven of knowledge in the face of harsh reality, exemplifies the human spirit's unwavering desire for study and peace. Within its book-lined halls, one can almost imagine captives taking solace in the pages of a well-worn novel, briefly escaping the limits of their reality.

Furthermore, historical reports of inmates offer stories of remarkable perseverance. Daring escapes, unexpected gestures of generosity, and the calm dignity with which many suffered their sentences all demonstrate humanity's resilience even within these merciless walls.

Stepping out of the penitentiary and out into the warm Idaho sunshine feels like a release, not only for the visitor, but also for a piece of history held within. The Old Idaho State Penitentiary is more than just a tourist attraction; it is a site for historical reflection. It compels us to confront the darkness of the past, to value freedom, and to remember the experiences of those who have walked these same grounds before us.

Sacajawea Interpretive, Cultural, and Educational Center

The Sacajawea Interpretive, Cultural, and Education Center, located in Idaho's Lemhi County, is an important resource for learning about Sacagawea, the Shoshone woman who had an indelible impact on the Lewis and Clark Expedition. A recent visit proved to be a wealth of information, providing a thorough examination of her story and the Shoshone-Bannock cultural tapestry.

The initial exhibit quickly transported visitors back in time. Through painstakingly arranged displays and informational panels, a vivid image of Shoshone-Bannock life formed. The walls were covered in intricate beadwork, with each geometric design and symbolic image telling a story about their artistic past. Traditional tools and weapons, constructed with skill and creativity, provide insight into their practical genius.

Moving farther into the centre, one comes to a life-size reproduction of a Shoshone house. This moving depiction of Sacagawea's early upbringing provided an insight into the houses she knew before joining the expedition. Stepping inside, the warmth of a crackling fire (created with expert lighting and storytelling) and the murmur of daily life presented a compelling picture. This display expertly integrated the practicality of daily life with the Shoshone-Bannock people's rich cultural heritage.

A very interesting piece focused on Sacagawea's early life. Visitors can learn about the dramatic events that occurred, including her captivity by the Hidatsa tribe, her subsequent absorption into their community, and, finally, her vital function as a guide and interpreter for Lewis and Clark. The weight of her obligation as a young lady put into unusual circumstances was overwhelming.

Interactive displays brought the Lewis and Clark Expedition to life in an engaging manner. Visitors could practically hear the crackling of Lewis and Clark's diaries as they read digital entries about their interactions with the

Shoshone-Bannock people. Sacagawea's critical role in travelling unknown lands, procuring food, and acting as a cultural bridge became glaringly obvious.

The centre promoted a high level of historical accuracy. Panellists recognized the intricacies of the expedition's influence on Native American tribes, such as the disruption to their way of life and the continued struggle for recognition of their achievements. This refreshing exhibition of candour prompted people to adopt a more nuanced view of history.

Stepping outside, one was immediately immersed in the same landscape that Sacagawea previously traversed. The centre's well-kept walking pathways wound through the gorgeous environs, with scheduled stops highlighting the plants and resources used by the Shoshone-Bannock people. Each designated location acted as a quiet tribute to Sacagawea's vast understanding of the natural world, improving the entire learning experience.

The Sacajawea Interpretive Center went beyond the scope of a typical museum. It served as a source of emotion, inspiring a renewed respect for Sacagawea's bravery, tenacity, and essential contribution to American history. The centre serves as a striking reminder that her legacy is considerably more than a footnote in a history book. It demonstrates the Shoshone-Bannock people's lasting spirit and their critical role in determining the trajectory of American discovery.

Cataldo Mission

Nestled among the undulating plains of northern Idaho, the Cataldo Mission stands out like a light from another era. Built in the late 18th century by Spanish missionaries and indigenous peoples, this masterfully preserved adobe structure provides a fascinating peek into Idaho's rich history. As I approached the goal, the weight of history became tangible. The sun-baked adobe bricks, infused with the warmth of countless summers, whispered stories of religion, cultural interchange, and community resilience.

Stepping Through Time

The hefty oak door creaked open, providing a refreshing respite from the afternoon heat. Inside, there was a tremendous aura of devotion. Sunlight flowed through the tall windows, casting lengthy shadows on the modest yet attractive interior. Worn wooden pews ringed the middle nave, their smooth surfaces hinting at the many prayers said and stories told. The remnants of the altar and baptismal font served as mute reminders of the mission's religious purpose.

A Center for Faith and Community

Our skilled guide, with a voice full of enthusiasm for Idaho history, brought the mission's history to life. The Cataldo Mission was more than just a place of prayer; it also served as an important centre for education and communal life. Spanish missionaries brought European farming skills and cattle to the indigenous Coeur d'Alene people, permanently changing their way of life. Through her perceptive narration, the walls seemed to echo with the sounds of the past, such as prayer chanting, lesson murmurs, and shared laughing and discussion.

A Story About Resilience

The Cataldo Mission's story is more than just one of religious devotion. It demonstrates incredible resiliency. A catastrophic earthquake in the nineteenth century levelled the structure. However, in the early twentieth century, a committed group of preservationists rose to the task. Driven by a strong admiration for Idaho's legacy, they set out on their own quest to meticulously restore this historical relic to its former glory. Today, the Cataldo Mission stands gloriously as a beacon of fortitude, a testament to the everlasting force of historic preservation.

A Window into the Past

Wandering through the renovated hallways of the Cataldo Mission provided a deep appreciation for Idaho's rich heritage. It promoted a better understanding of the various civilizations that have produced this lovely state. When I stepped outdoors, the carefully maintained grounds spread in front of me, tempting me to explore more. A reconstructed granary stood sentinel, a tangible reminder of agricultural techniques from centuries past. The soft murmur of Potlatch Creek, a permanent presence throughout the mission's history, served as a tranquil backdrop to the scenario.

A Lasting Legacy

As I left the Cataldo Mission, the golden hues of evening bathed the countryside in warm tones. The beautiful silence was disturbed only by crickets chirping and the gentle sighing of the breeze. Nonetheless, stories reverberated within the mission's holy walls. The Cataldo Mission is much more than just a historical site. It is a vivid monument to the enduring human spirit, the power of faith and community, and a glimpse into Idaho's unique history.

Minidoka National Historic Site

The wind whispers across the parched plains of southern Idaho, bringing with it memories of a turbulent past. The Minidoka National Historic Site stands out against the austere grandeur of the desert terrain as a haunting reminder of a chapter in American history that should not be forgotten. This immaculately conserved old correctional institution invites visitors on a voyage of discovery and introspection.

When you enter the visitor centre, you will find a wealth of information. Interactive exhibits and informational displays provide a realistic depiction of the Japanese American Exclusion Order, a dark stain on American soil. During World War II, more than 120,000 Japanese Americans, many of whom were US citizens, were forcibly removed from their homes on the West Coast and imprisoned in camps around the country. Minidoka, once a thriving town, has become an unusual home to almost 13,000 people.

Walking inside the restored barracks provides a palpable connection to the past. The modest, plain buildings serve as quiet testaments to the terrible reality of captivity. Tiny chambers designed to hold entire families say much about the internees' inadequate living conditions. Exhibits shed light on their daily lives, highlighting the restricted rations and repetitive food that provided their subsistence.

However, Minidoka's narrative goes beyond hardship. The human spirit persevered within the camp's limits. Exhibits highlight the internees' amazing perseverance and resourcefulness. Schools were built, businesses sprouted up, and even newspapers circulated, establishing a sense of normalcy and belonging. Photographs depict vivid cultural festivities, demonstrating the enduring spirit of people who were wrongfully imprisoned.

The harsh beauty of the surrounding desert is key to understanding the Minidoka experience. Consider the enormous emptiness that stretched before the internees' gaze, a continual reminder of their solitude. Nonetheless, the desert provided a space for solitary contemplation and connectedness to the natural world, in stark contrast to the constraints of the camp.

A visit to the Block 21 Relocation Center Cemetery is a powerful reminder of the human cost of fear and prejudice. Rows of plain headstones lie silently, each representing a life cut short within the boundaries of the camp. Amidst the silence, one can not help but think of the dreadful repercussions of bigotry.

The Minidoka National Historic Site goes beyond its status as a historical landmark. It is a tremendous monument to the human spirit's ability to overcome adversity, as well as a harsh reminder of the significance of combating all types of discrimination and prejudice. By learning from previous failures, we can work toward a future in which similar injustices do not occur again. Leaving the grounds, one has a fresh respect for the liberties we value, as well as a resolve to create a more inclusive and just society.

Chapter 4: Experiencing Idaho's Local Life

Huckleberry picking in the Sawtooth National Forest

The fresh mountain air energised my senses, bearing the distinct sweetness of ripe huckleberries. Sunlight dappled through the lodgepole pines, creating a captivating play of light and shadow on the forest floor. Nestled amidst the rugged splendour of the Sawtooth National Forest, a ritual as ancient as the mountains themselves unfolds: the hunt for these delightful purple gems.

The city's cacophony had faded, replaced by the melodious symphony of unseen songbirds and the rhythmic crunch of my boots on the well-worn trail. Eager anticipation, a familiar sense that becomes stronger with each successive year, simmered within me. Huckleberry picking in Idaho is more than just collecting berries; it is a full-sensory experience that allows you to reconnect with nature, make lasting memories, and harvest the abundance of the land.

I walked deeper into the jungle, armed with a strong bucket and a neatly marked map that had been passed down through generations. My eyes scoured the terrain, looking for the telltale signs: low-lying shrubs decorated with clusters of luscious, ripe huckleberries. Years of practice have improved my talents; optimal hunting grounds are locations with dappled sunshine, where these berries thrive. Then, a triumphant find! A bright patch of purple tucked among the emerald foliage. As I carefully knelt, plucking each huckleberry with trained precision, ensuring minimal harm to the fragile bushes, a rush of joy passed through me.

As I carefully filled my bucket, the calm of the woodland engulfed me. The rhythmic whisper of leaves moving in the breeze, and the distant gurgle of a hidden brook, were the only sounds that broke the tranquil silence. Time appeared to slip away as I became entirely immersed in the task at hand. Huckleberry picking is more than just picking berries; it is about slowing down, appreciating the simple beauty of the natural world, and basking in the satisfaction of a successful harvest.

Throughout my investigations, I met other huckleberry enthusiasts. We swapped stories, engaged in lighthearted competition over the finest picking places (always tightly kept secrets!), and nurtured the camaraderie that comes with participating in a beloved tradition. Laughter reverberated through the trees as we compared our harvests, each with a bucket brimming with the prized berries.

However, the actual joy of huckleberry picking is the prospect of future culinary delights. The prospect of transforming these little purple jewels into wonderful sweets like huckleberry pies with golden-brown crusts, fluffy huckleberry pancakes, or jars of homemade huckleberry jam increased my enthusiasm. The act of picking serves as a forerunner to creating delightful memories with loved ones at the table.

As the day progressed, my bucket filled with luscious, juicy huckleberries. A sense of accomplishment washed over me, along with a welcome exhaustion from hours spent in the majestic majesty of the Sawtooths. I left the forest with more than just a wealth of berries; I carried the tranquillity of the mountains, the excitement of the hunt, and the promise of future culinary delights.

Huckleberry picking in the Sawtooth National Forest is more than just a recreational pastime; it is a cultural touchstone, a chance to connect with the land and previous generations. It reminds us of the simple pleasures in life, the satisfaction of self-reliance, and the innate wealth that nature provides. So, if your travels take you to Idaho during huckleberry season, I recommend that you grab a bucket and head into the wild. You might just come into a hidden gem, not in the form of a delectable berry, but in the changing experience itself.

Explore Idaho's Artisan Beer Scene

Idaho's stunning scenery are not the only things that will satisfy your need for adventure. The "Gem State" is home to a thriving craft beer culture, full of innovative brewers, distinct flavour characteristics, and a welcoming community attitude. Whether you are a seasoned hophead or a curious newcomer, Idaho's craft beer culture provides an amazing experience.

A Thriving Foamy Frontier

While Idaho's craft beer culture may not be the first to come to mind, its past is surprisingly rich. In the late 1980s, microbreweries such as Suds Brothers Brewing in Coeur d'Alene and Great Basin Brewing Company in Boise emerged, paving the way for a more diverse and tasty future. Today, the state is home to over 100 breweries, each with its own unique narrative to tell and a passion for creating outstanding beer.

A Brewers Paradise

Idaho's diversified terrain leads to a wonderfully wide beer choice. From rich barley fields to pristine alpine streams, the state provides an ideal base for a wide range of styles. Here's a look at some of the important brewing regions:

Boise

Idaho's capital city serves as a starting point for your craft beer excursion. Begin at Boise Brewing, a founding father of the state's beer sector, and try their classic Publican Pale Ale. Crooked Lane Brewing creates unique sour beers, while Payette Brewing produces award-winning IPAs that highlight the bright citrus aromas of locally grown hops.

Sun Valley and Central Idaho

Looking for a more casual vibe? Sun Valley Brewing greets you with spectacular mountain vistas and delicious beers. Head north to Sawtooth Brewery in Hailey, which is known for its award-winning oatmeal stout. Do not miss Salmon River Brewing in Salmon, where the Huckleberry Hefeweizen showcases the region's wild abundance.

Eastern Idaho

Snake River Brewing in Idaho Falls is known for their creative and innovative brews, which will please craft beer fans. Further east, Grand Teton Brewing in Jackson Hole offers Teton Ale, an ideal partner for visiting the spectacular Teton Range.

Beyond The Pint

Idaho's artisan beer scene extends beyond the liquid gold itself. Breweries frequently morph into active neighbourhood gathering places, including live music, trivia nights, and even board game nights. This creates a welcome environment for both residents and visitors to meet and share their passion for craft beer.

Become a Craft Beer Connoisseur

Plan your Pilgrimage

Plan a path through the breweries in your chosen regions. Many cities and areas offer brewery tours, which allow you to try a variety of selections in an effective manner. Consider getting a brewery passport that includes discounts and even awards for visiting a certain number of breweries.

Sample Responsibly

Most breweries provide flights, which allow you to sample multiple beers in smaller servings. This is a great way to try new cuisines and find your favourites. Always remember to pace yourself and assign a driver when visiting different venues.

Support Local

Growlers and crowlers are easily available at numerous breweries, allowing you to bring a taste of Idaho home. Buying products like t-shirts and hats demonstrates your support for these local businesses.

Engage with the Brewers

Intrigued by the brewing process? Ask questions! Interact with the brewers about their techniques, ingredients, and inspiration for each beer. You may receive priceless insights and a renewed appreciation for the craft.

Savour the Experience

Craft beer is about savouring the full trip. Relax, absorb up the environment, and enjoy the effort and love that went into each sip. Idaho's craft beer scene, with its wide products, friendly communities, and commitment to quality, is primed to become your next hop-filled journey.

Visit Idaho's Local Farmers Markets

Idaho's agricultural legacy is highlighted by its strong network of farmers markets. These lively markets provide more than just fresh produce; they are a window into the heart of the state's culture, a celebration of local bounty, and a joyful experience for all visitors.

A Feast for the Senses

Stepping into an Idaho farmers market immerses you immediately in a symphony of sights, smells, and noises. Towering displays of ruby red tomatoes and emerald green zucchinis create a rainbow of colours. The air is alive with friendly talk, and the seductive aromas of freshly made bread mix with the earthy perfume of locally cultivated herbs. Lush bouquets of sunflowers and scented lavender add beauty, while a local musician's rhythmic strumming serves as a lively backdrop.

Connecting with the Land and its Stewards

Beyond the visual feast, there is the opportunity to meet with the farmers themselves. These dedicated citizens, custodians of Idaho's fertile land, proudly display their harvest. Each stall tells a narrative of attentive care, overcoming seasonal hurdles, and having a strong respect for the environment. Engaging with them provides more than just an instructive interaction; it also allows you to appreciate the effort that goes into your cuisine. Learn about unique heirloom types, regional specialties, and professional tips for picking the ripest peaches and juiciest melons. This intimate relationship inspires a renewed appreciation for Idaho's agricultural backbone.

A Treasure Trove of Local Delights

Idaho's farmers markets go well beyond fruits and vegetables. They are brimming with locally produced gems. Explore an artisan's collection of hand-knitted wool scarves, complex wood sculptures, and humorous pottery items. Discover the golden glimmer of local honey, a monument to the hard work of Idaho's beekeeping community. Enjoy the brilliant colours and tantalising fragrances of home-baked pies, jams, and jellies, each a delectable expression of Idaho's culinary tradition. Many markets also have prepared food vendors that sell sizzling tamales, savoury quiches, and sweet pastries, allowing you to enjoy the region's characteristics in a delicious mouthful. Here, supporting local companies goes hand in hand with having a culinary adventure.

More than just a Marketplace

The essential core of Idaho's farmers markets is their capacity to generate a sense of community. Families walk hand in hand, youngsters point out beautiful produce, lively conversations float through the crowd, and local musicians serenade the customers. It is a place where visitors and residents may meet, bonding over a love of fresh, local delicacies and handcrafted goods. Grab a cup of freshly brewed coffee or a drink of local cider and enjoy the lively atmosphere. You are more than a tourist here; you are a part of Idaho's vivid tapestry of life.

Maximise Your Market Experience

To thoroughly enjoy the farmers market experience, visit early to get the best assortment of produce. Bring reusable bags to reduce your environmental effect and consider carrying cash, though many vendors accept credit cards as well. Do not be afraid to engage with the farmers and craftspeople, ask questions, and try a bite (with permission, of course!).

A Lasting Impression

A visit to an Idaho farmers market is more than simply a shopping experience; it is an engaging journey through the state's agricultural core. It is an opportunity to connect with the land, the people who work it, and the spirit of Idaho itself. So, on your next Idaho adventure, make sure to visit a local farmers market. Allow the bright colours, cheerful chats, and plenty of fresh fruit to leave a memorable image of your journey.

Native American Cultural Experiences in Idaho

Idaho's stunning landscapes have a deep history, linked together by the enduring spirit of the Native American tribes who have lived here for millennia. Idaho, home to the Shoshone-Bannock people, the Nez Perce, and the Coeur d'Alene tribes, provides a unique opportunity to connect with these vibrant cultures and develop a deeper understanding of their legacy. This guide delves into some unique experiences that will deepen your awareness of Idaho's Native American tapestry.

Immersion Through Cultural Centers

The Sacajawea Interpretive, Cultural, and Education Center in Lemhi County is a good place to start learning about Idaho's Native American past. Sacagawea's life and legacy are brought to life here through expertly organised exhibitions. Visitors can learn about her tenacity, resourcefulness, and the critical role she made to the expedition's success. The centre goes on to showcase the Shoshone-Bannock people's traditional way of life, including displays on their hunting and gathering activities, elaborate beading artistry, and the rich symbolism woven into their clothes and implements.

The Power of Storytelling
The Coeur d'Alene Tribal Museum provides a fascinating experience. Visitors can experience the power of storytelling firsthand. Tribal elders, their voices full of tradition, recall the Coeur

d'Alene people's history, their strong connection to the land, and the ideals that have guided them for decades. The museum walls serve as a canvas for elaborate beadwork, with each design conveying a tale and each hue representing a specific significance. Visitors learn about the significance of salmon in Coeur d'Alene culture, as well as the precise fishing skills that have been passed down through the generations. A visit around the museum is like entering into a live tapestry of Coeur d'Alene history.

Witnessing the Powwow's Thundering Spirit

Going to a powwow is an unforgettable experience. As you enter the designated area, you can feel the vivid energy. The rhythmic pounding of drums reverberates throughout the area, a powerful heartbeat that connects dancers to their ancestors and the earth. Dancers in brilliant regalia take centre stage, with each feather, bead, and complex design representing their heritage and stories. Witnessing a powwow is more than simply entertainment; it is a celebration of community, a reaffirmation of cultural identity, and a strong manifestation of Native Americans' enduring spirit.

Learning Through Hands-on Experiences

Many tribes offer educational workshops that go further into their traditions. Visitors may attend a workshop on traditional basket making with a Shoshone-Bannock craftsman. Her hands, seasoned yet nimble, carefully guide participants through the steps of picking willow branches, soaking them, and weaving them into a beautiful and functional basket. With each stage, she tells stories about the craft's significance, the symbolism embedded in the patterns, and the holy connection between the basket and the natural world.

Respectful Engagement with Local Artists

Contemporary Native American artists' works are on display at art galleries and shops around Idaho. Intricate beading covers everything from jewellery to clothing, with each piece demonstrating the creator's ability and artistic vision. Visitors can interact with these artists and learn about the inspiration for their work. A young Nez Perce artist might explain how her beautiful landscapes are filled with ancestral stories. Buying art becomes more than just a souvenir; it is a means to support these artists' livelihoods while also bringing a bit of their culture home.

A Journey of Respect and Connection

Exploring Native American traditions in Idaho is a rewarding and humbling experience. It serves as a reminder of these communities' strong connection to the land, the value of storytelling in conserving traditions, and the cultures' enduring spirit. As you embark on your adventure, remember to be a courteous guest. Respect tribal grounds, obtain permission before photographing, and attend traditional activities with an open mind and want to learn. By participating with these dynamic cultures, you will obtain a better knowledge of Idaho's complex tapestry and make memories that will last long after your trip is over.

Chapter 5: Practical Information for Travelers in Idaho

Accommodation Options in Idaho

As you begin your Idaho adventure, your chosen lodging will serve as your sanctuary, a place to relax and recharge after a day of visiting the state's diverse landscapes and rich cultural tapestry. This book explores the various lodging alternatives accessible in Idaho, appealing to every taste and budget, providing a pleasant and memorable stay.

Immerse yourself in Nature

Camping provides a memorable experience for the adventurous tourist looking for an unrivalled connection to nature. Imagine waking up to the fresh mountain air, birds chirping as your only alarm clock, and stunning scenery spreading before your tent. Idaho has a plethora of campgrounds spread around the state, from national forests to state parks, allowing you to locate the ideal location to pitch your tent or park your RV.

National Forest Campgrounds

National forest campgrounds, nestled among towering pines or bordered by scenic lakes, offer a modest yet enjoyable experience. Picnic tables, fire rings, and, on occasion, vault toilets are among these. Surrounded by the grandeur of nature, you will experience starlit nights and an amazing symphony of wildlife sounds.

State Park Campgrounds

State parks typically provide more services, such as showers, laundry facilities, and even camp stores supplied with supplies. Many include breathtaking natural features such as waterfalls, canyons, or access to lakes, ideal for swimming, boating, and fishing.

Glamping with Style

Glamping is the excellent alternative for individuals who want to connect with nature while yet feeling comfortable. Consider comfortable yurts, well-appointed cabins, or even magnificent tents complete with plush bedding and amenities such as private decks and fire pits. Glamping locations frequently have common areas such as fire pits and outdoor seating, which fosters a sense of community while still letting you connect with the natural world.

Embrace Western Hospitality

A dude ranch offers a true cowboy experience. These historic ranches provide a distinct blend of rustic charm and modern amenities. Expect cosy cabins or lodge rooms, substantial home-cooked meals, and a variety of activities that capture the essence of the West. Saddle up for horseback riding experiences, learn how to fly fish, take part in cattle drives (depending on the season), or simply relax by a crackling campfire beneath a starry sky.

Bed & Breakfasts

Consider staying at a bed and breakfast. These quaint inns, which are often housed in old buildings, provide a warm and welcoming environment. Imagine waking up to the aroma of freshly baked bread, sharing a delicious handmade breakfast with your fellow tourists, and exchanging stories with the friendly innkeepers who can offer insider ideas for visiting the area.

Hotels & Motels

Idaho has a variety of hotels and motels at various pricing points for visitors looking for a comfortable and convenient stay. Whether you want a low-cost hotel with basic amenities or a luxurious hotel with expensive amenities such as spas, fitness centres, and on-site restaurants, you will find an option that meets your needs. These facilities are frequently located near major attractions and provide convenient access to dining and shopping opportunities.

Vacation Rentals

Vacation rentals are an appealing option for families, groups of friends, and tourists looking for big and private accommodations. Choose from modest cabins secluded in the woods or huge holiday homes on the banks of picturesque lakes. These rentals frequently include fully equipped kitchens, living areas, and various bedrooms, allowing you to stretch out, cook your own meals, and make unforgettable moments together.

Immerse yourself in Local Flavour

Some of Idaho's unique lodging alternatives offer an exceptional experience. Imagine sleeping in a historic fire lookout tower perched atop a mountain peak, with stunning panoramic views. Stay in a lovely treehouse tucked among the branches of tall trees, ideal for a romantic retreat or a spectacular excursion for family. Consider glamping in a converted sheep wagon, a symbol of Idaho's ranching tradition.

Book Your Ideal Accommodation

Consider these helpful recommendations to acquire the ideal accommodations for your Idaho adventure:

Plan Beforehand

Popular sites, especially during peak seasons (summer and winter), tend to fill up rapidly. Make your reservations well in advance, especially if you have your heart set on a specific location or style of accommodation.

Consider the Season

Camping may be perfect for a summer vacation, but it is not recommended during the hard winter months. Choose your accommodation according to the season. During the winter, pleasant cabins or hotels with fireplaces are more appealing. To guarantee a comfortable stay, research the weather conditions in your preferred destinations.

Budget

Idaho has a number of solutions to suit different budgets. Camping and hostels are the most affordable options, while luxury hotels and dude ranches provide premium experiences. Determine your daily spending limit and select an accommodation that fits within your financial comfort zone.

Location, Location, Location

Consider your itinerary and preferred level of proximity to attractions. If you intend to spend the majority of your time outside, a campsite near your scheduled activities could be great. Staying at a centrally placed hotel allows you to visit lively towns and cities with ease.

Amenities

Make a note of what amenities are important to you. Do you need Wi-Fi, laundry facilities, or on-site dining? Some campgrounds include basic amenities such as restrooms and showers, while others are very primitive. Glamping and vacation rentals frequently have kitchens for self-catering, whereas hotels may offer room service or on-site eateries.

Read Reviews

Use internet travel platforms and guidebooks to read evaluations from past visitors. This can provide vital information about the overall experience, cleanliness, and amenities provided by various lodgings.

Embrace the Unexpected

Sometimes the most unforgettable events come from the unexpected. If your preferred accommodation is fully booked, be willing to consider different possibilities. You might come across a nice B&B or a cosy cabin that provides an unexpected treat.

Unforgettable Experiences

Your lodging should not only be a place to sleep. Many Idaho accommodation alternatives provide unique experiences that might help you enjoy your trip. Here are a few instances.

Dude Ranches

These functioning ranches offer the opportunity to learn about cowboy culture, participate in cattle drives (season allowing), and improve your horseback riding skills. Some even include guided walks, fishing expeditions, and campfire storytelling sessions under the starry sky.

Bed & Breakfasts

Many B&Bs have on-site gardens or offer cooking workshops, so you may learn about local foods and traditional dishes. Some may even organise wine tastings or cultural evenings, providing a deeper look into Idaho's history.

Unique Stays

Treehouse rentals may have stargazing chances or private terraces ideal for enjoying morning coffee amidst the whispering foliage. Sleeping aboard a converted sheep wagon may include ranch visits and campfire conversations about Idaho's ranching history.

By selecting the correct accommodations and taking advantage of the unique experiences provided by your lodging facility, you can ensure that your Idaho adventure is more than simply a holiday but an amazing journey of discovery.

Transportation in the State

Welcome to Idaho, the "Gem State"! Idaho's diverse landscapes, ranging from harsh mountains to huge deserts, provide ample chances for adventure. However, before embarking on your trip, you must first learn how to move around. This book delves into the numerous transportation alternatives accessible in the state, ensuring a comfortable and enjoyable journey.

Car Rental and Scenic Drives

For many travellers, the freedom of the open road means renting a car. This choice opens up a world of options, allowing you to create a personalised schedule and explore at your own speed.

Scenic Byways

Take a self-guided adventure along Idaho's stunning scenic highways. Explore breathtaking mountains, pristine lakes, and enormous expanses of high desert. Cruise down the Kelly Canyon Scenic Byway for panoramic views of the Sawtooth Mountains, or meander down the Selway-Bittersweet Scenic Byway, which is known for its vivid wildflower displays and unique wildlife interactions.

Flexibility

A rented car gives you the most flexibility. Spontaneous trips to lovely roadside sights or picnics beside isolated lakes become simple options. This level of liberty allows you to make the most of your exploring time and adapt your trip to your own preferences.

Cost Effectiveness (for groups)

When compared to individual public transportation prices, renting a car as a group can be a more cost-effective option. Additionally, owning your own transportation minimises reliance on public transportation timetables, allowing for more efficient travel between destinations.

Important Tips for a Smooth Car Journey

Driver's Licence

Ensure you have a valid driver's licence. International travellers may be required to obtain an international driving permit.

Car Rental Reservations

To minimise last-minute availability concerns, book your rental car ahead of time, especially during peak season.

Navigation

While GPS navigation is widely available, having a hardcopy map as a backup is strongly advised, especially in isolated locations with minimal cell coverage.

Road Condition Awareness

Stay educated about road conditions, especially during the winter months when snow and ice can create hazardous driving conditions. If you plan to go to snowy areas, be sure your car has winter requirements such as snow tires and chains.

Gas Station Planning

Gas stations may be scarce in some remote locations. Fill up your tank whenever possible, particularly before leaving major towns or cities.

Exploring Public Transport Options

If you want a hands-off travel experience or do not own a car, Idaho has public transit choices, which are mostly centred in major cities. This is an overview:

City Buses

Larger cities, such as Boise, Pocatello, and Idaho Falls, have well-developed public bus systems that provide efficient and cheap methods to travel their metropolitan environments. Consider purchasing day passes or pre-paid tickets to potentially save money.

Intercity Buses

Some of Idaho's major cities are connected by limited intercity buses. Greyhound offers routes throughout the state, connecting bigger towns and neighbouring areas. To secure your seat, check the schedule and book your tickets ahead of time.

Trains

Amtrak provides little passenger train service inside Idaho. The Empire Builder road runs through the northern half of the state, offering picturesque drives with stops in Sandpoint and Spokane, Washington (just across the border).

While public transit options may be limited in some areas, they can be an effective way to explore cities or get to major transportation hubs where you can rent a car.

Ferries and Boat Tours

Idaho's pristine lakes and scenic rivers provide unique vacation experiences. Consider the following possibilities for exploring the situation from a different perspective:

Ferries

Several ferry services traverse significant lakes such as Lake Coeur d'Alene and Priest Lake, linking cities and providing breathtaking views of the surrounding surroundings. Relax and enjoy the view as you cross the lake, giving a fresh twist to your journey.

Boat Tours

Join a boat excursion to get up close and personal with some of Idaho's most spectacular natural treasures. A thrilling jet boat excursion allows you to explore Hells Canyon National Recreation Area's stunning cliffs and hidden coves. Take a leisurely boat on Lake Coeur d'Alene, admiring the splendour of the surrounding mountains and spotting majestic bald eagles soaring above.

Alternative Modes of Transportation

Idaho provides intriguing alternative transportation possibilities for the genuinely adventurous tourist.

Biking

Idaho has a vast network of attractive bike lanes and tough terrain. Rent a bike and explore the Boise River Greenbelt, a paved pathway that runs through the city's heart, or take on the epic Trail of the Coeur d'Alenes, a 51-mile paved rails-to-trails road that passes through stunning countryside.

Horseback Riding

Explore Idaho's backcountry on horseback to get in touch with your inner cowboy. Many dude ranches and outfitters provide guided horseback riding trips, allowing you to explore gorgeous trails while connecting with the state's ranching tradition.

Hiking

Lace up your boots and hit the trail! Idaho is a hiker's dream, with endless paths suitable for all ability levels. Explore Sawtooth National Recreation Area's alpine meadows and glacial lakes, or take on the difficult switchbacks of Hells Canyon National Recreation Area's Grady Creek Trail.

Choosing Your Ideal Transportation

Your travel style, itinerary, and money will all influence which mode of transportation is best for your Idaho journey. Here are some concluding remarks to help you decide:

Adventurous Spirit

For the adventurous traveller, vehicle rentals, bikes, and even horseback riding open up a world of adventure possibilities.

Budget-Conscious

Public transportation in urban areas and carpooling with other travellers can be cost-effective choices.

Relaxation and Convenience

If you prefer a hands-off travel experience and want to take in the sights without having to navigate, consider guided tours, ferries, or even rail journeys.

Essential Travel Tips

Here are some helpful ideas to help you navigate Idaho smoothly:

Map and Navigation Apps

Invest in a printed map of Idaho and download dependable navigation applications on your phone as backup. Cell service may be limited in rural regions.

Weather Awareness

Be careful of weather conditions, especially during the winter months, when snow and ice can cause road closures and travel delays. Pack clothing and supplies based on the expected weather in your chosen places.

Respecting the Environment

Whether driving, cycling, or trekking, practise responsible travel by reducing your environmental effect. Dispose of rubbish correctly, do not disturb wildlife, and leave no trace.

By selecting the most appropriate mode of transportation and following these vital suggestions, you can turn your trip from point A to point B into an amazing adventure that allows you to discover the true spirit of the "Gem State."

Shopping Tips and Recommendations

Idaho's allure extends beyond its breathtaking landscapes and vibrant cultures; nestled within charming towns and bustling cities lies a shopper's paradise. This curated guide delves into the diverse retail scene, empowering you to discover unique treasures, locally crafted goods, and authentic souvenirs that encapsulate the essence of the Gem State.

Supporting Local Artisanship

Idaho has a robust artistic scene; here's where to find their creations:

Art Gallery and Studio

Explore galleries in Boise, Coeur d'Alene, and Sun Valley to immerse yourself in the artistic spirit and discover captivating paintings, sculptures, ceramics, and exquisite jewellery. Often, you can meet the artists themselves and gain a deeper appreciation for their creative process and stories behind each piece.

Farmers' Markets

Beyond fresh produce, many markets display homemade objects, such as delicately woven baskets, hand-painted pottery, and wonderfully created woodwork. Engage in discussion with the craftspeople, who frequently give intriguing stories about their creations.

Craft Fairs and Festivals

Throughout the year, vibrant craft fairs and festivals erupt across the state, immersing you in the festive atmosphere and losing yourself in a treasure trove of handcrafted goods. From handmade quilts and knitted scarves to hand-carved wooden toys and locally blended soaps, you will find unique items that perfectly capture the essence of Idaho.

Souvenirs With Authentic Charm

To get a sense of the Wild West, look for shops that specialise in Western-themed items.

Western Wear Stores

Step back in time and discover authentic cowboy hats, sturdy boots, and beautiful belts that capture the spirit of the frontier. These useful pieces may also become treasured memories, bringing a bit of Western flair to your outfit.

Trading Posts and Gift Shop

Tourist sites frequently have quaint trading posts and gift shops stocked with items that pay respect to Idaho's history and legacy, including postcards showcasing breathtaking vistas, keychains with the distinctive state logo, and warm t-shirts embroidered with smart Idaho slogans.

Antique Stores and Flea Markets

Discover vintage treasures like faded cowboy boots, antique spurs, or even old photographs portraying Idaho's rich past, which can serve as conversation starters and treasured recollections of your excursions.

Culinary Delights To Take Home

Do not pass up the opportunity to enjoy Idaho's wonderful treats:

Candy Stores

Indulge your inner child by visiting a candy store and sampling famous huckleberry candies, which range from chewy gummies to rich chocolates flavoured with this unique local berry. Stock up on these sweet delights for yourself or take a bag home as a delectable keepsake.

Chocolate Shops

Indulge in decadent chocolates crafted by local chocolatiers. From creamy truffles to hand-dipped pretzels, these shops offer a variety of treats to satisfy any sweet tooth. Do not miss out on locally-sourced flavours like huckleberry and marionberry, which add a unique Idaho twist to your chocolate fix.

Farmers Markets and Local Grocers

Explore the abundance of Idaho's farms and orchards. Stock up on local honey, jams and jellies overflowing with fresh fruit tastes, and artisan cheeses for a gourmet spread back home. These tasty keepsakes encapsulate the essence of Idaho's agricultural legacy and will be appreciated long after your visit.

Pro Tips for Savvy Shoppers

Maximise your shopping adventures in Idaho with these insider tips:

Haggling

While haggling is uncommon, it is often allowed at flea markets and antique shops. Inquire politely about a reduced price, especially if you intend to purchase numerous items.

Cash vs. Cards

Most larger stores and restaurants accept major credit and debit cards, but some smaller shops and vendors may only accept cash, so keep some dollars on hand.

Tax-free Shopping

Fortunately, Idaho has no state sales tax, so you only pay taxes based on the local sales tax rate in the city or county you are shopping in. This makes Idaho a paradise for frugal shoppers seeking for great discounts.

Packing Light

While the desire to buy everything you see is powerful, try travelling light. Many establishments have online sites, allowing you to explore your favourite findings when you return home.

By following these suggestions and stepping beyond souvenir shops, you will discover gems that capture the essence of Idaho and create lasting memories of your trip across the Gem State.

Currency and Payment Methods

A smooth financial experience is essential for a successful trip, and this guide goes into the realm of currencies and payment methods available in Idaho, allowing you to manage transactions with confidence.

The Universal Standard

From bustling city centres to isolated gas stations, businesses in Idaho routinely take crisp banknotes, jingling coins, and traveller's cheques denominated in US dollars (USD).

Credit and Debit Cards

Major credit cards, such as Visa, Mastercard, and American Express, are widely accepted across the state, providing a convenient and secure way to pay for goods and services. Debit cards with ATM access provide even more flexibility, allowing for cash withdrawals at conveniently located ATMs in most towns and cities.

Considerations for Using Cards

Foreign Transaction Fees

International travellers should inquire about any foreign transaction costs linked with using their cards overseas. Choosing cards with no such fees can help you maximise your budget.

Chip and Pin Technology

Many Idaho establishments have embraced chip and PIN technology for increased security; ensure that your cards are chip-enabled and that you know your Personal Identification Number (PIN) for faster transactions.

Limited Cell Service

While most urban areas have adequate mobile coverage, heading into isolated locations may leave you disconnected. Carrying backup funds ensures that you are prepared for any eventuality.

The Persistent Value of Cash

Despite the dominance of plastic, cash is still important in certain situations:

Small Towns and Rural Areas

Some smaller towns and rural shops have limited card processing capabilities, so keeping cash on hand helps you to support local economies by purchasing crafts, eating at lovely eateries, or filling up on necessities at general stores.

Tipping

Tipping service providers, such as servers, bartenders, and taxi drivers, is common in the United States. While some restaurants may allow you to add a tip to your credit card bill, having cash allows you to tip on the spot.

Entrance Fees and Vending Machines

National and state parks, as well as some historical sites, frequently levy admission fees collected at cash-only booths. Similarly, vending machines and public restrooms that need a nominal cost usually operate on a cash-only basis.

Exchange Currency for International Travelers

If you are travelling from outside the United States, consider converting some of your home currency for USD before your trip. Here are several options:

Exchange at Your Home Bank

Exchanging a modest amount at your home bank prior to leaving ensures that you have fast access to USD when you arrive.

Airport Currency Exchange

Although airport currency exchange kiosks are convenient, they frequently provide less favourable rates, so use them as a last alternative for little quantities.

ATMs in Idaho

Check with your bank about any ATM withdrawal fees that may apply when using your card abroad, as most Idaho ATMs only accept USD.

Essential Advice for a Secure Financial Journey

Inform your Bank

Notify your bank of your travel intentions ahead of time to avoid potential card usage concerns caused by suspected fraudulent behaviour.

Carry a Mixture

Maintain a balanced approach by carrying both cash and credit cards, ensuring preparedness for every occasion, whether it is a lovely cash-only business or a sophisticated restaurant with cutting-edge payment technology.

Budget Wisely

Set a realistic budget for your vacation and keep track of your expenditures to avoid overpaying and ensure you have enough money to last the entire time of your excursion.

Understanding these vital insights and following these essential guidelines will enable you to confidently handle your financial transactions in Idaho, allowing you to focus on creating memorable memories in the "Gem State."

Chapter 6: Day Trips from Major Idaho Cities

Sawtooth Wilderness from Boise

Boise, Idaho's vibrant capital, has a plethora of metropolitan attractions. However, a short journey west reveals another paradise: the Sawtooth Wilderness. This rough region, known for its alpine lakes, snow-capped peaks, and brilliant wildflower meadows, entices outdoor enthusiasts with its breathtaking natural splendour. This guide describes a wonderful one-day trip from Boise to the Sawtooth Wilderness, preparing you for an unforgettable journey.

The Enticing Journey (About 2-3 Hours)

The travel from Boise to the Sawtooth Wilderness takes place along a picturesque highway, turning a routine commute into a visual show. Rolling countryside gradually gives way to towering pines, and the crisp air awakens your senses. As you approach Stanley, the picturesque gateway town to the forest, keep a look out for wildlife sightings, which include deer, elk, and even bald eagles.

Preparation is Key

Before travelling into the bush, be sure you have the right equipment. It is vital to have sturdy hiking boots, weather-appropriate breathable clothing, a refillable water bottle, plenty of snacks, sunscreen, bug repellant, and a camera to capture the spectacular view. Additionally, acquiring a National Forest Day Pass or Annual Pass provides access to designated trailheads.

Tailoring Your Adventure

The Sawtooth Wilderness welcomes hikers of all ability levels, with a broad range of paths. Here are several common alternatives, each with unique rewards:

Redfish Lake Loop (moderate, 3–4 hours)

This picturesque circular trail around crystal-clear Redfish Lake provides the quintessential Sawtooth experience. Wildflowers cover the meadows in vivid colours, while beautiful peaks are mirrored on the lake's surface. Look out for playful otters frolicking in the water.

Sawtooth Saddle (Strenuous, 5-7 hours)

Experienced hikers looking for stunning views will find this hard trek rewarding. Conquer steep inclines and slopes to be rewarded with breathtaking views of the entire Sawtooth Valley, straight out of a postcard.

Fish Creek Trail (Easy to Moderate; 2-3 hours)

This family-friendly trail runs alongside Fish Creek and provides a pleasant stroll through a verdant woodland. Cascading waterfalls and bright wildflowers provide an idyllic scene for a leisurely stroll.

A Respite in Stanley

After your climb, rest and recharge in the picturesque town of Stanley. Enjoy a hearty lunch at a local restaurant, a scoop of huckleberry ice cream (a local favourite), or a stroll around art galleries displaying regional talent.

Optional Activities

RedFish Lake Lodge

This old lodge, set on the lakeshore, provides picturesque boat cruises. Relax and observe the Sawtooth Valley from a fresh angle. Reservations are often advised.

Whitewater Rafting

Unleash your inner adventurer with a spectacular whitewater rafting trip down the Salmon River. Navigate rapids and take in the splendour of the Sawtooth Valley to witness nature's strength. (Prior booking with a respected outfitter is customary.)

Fishing

Cast your line into one of the crystal-clear lakes or raging rivers. The Sawtooth Wilderness has a strong trout population, providing an opportunity to interact with nature while maybe catching meals. (A valid Idaho fishing licence is necessary.)

A Serene Return

Leaving the Sawtooth Wilderness behind could be bittersweet. However, when you return to Boise, reflect on your day's adventures. The towering peaks, peaceful lakes, and invigorating mountain air will stay with you, enticing you back to explore nature more.

Essential Tips for a Successful Day Trip

Early Start

Extend your time in the woods by departing Boise early. Plan an early morning departure to avoid crowds and afternoon heat, especially during peak season.

Weather Awareness

Be aware of the weather forecast. Mountain weather can change quickly, so pack layers and be ready for unexpected rain showers.

Pack a Picnic Lunch

Pack a delicious and nutritious picnic lunch to fuel your excursion. Choose snacks that are lightweight and will give you consistent energy throughout your hike.

Leave No Trace

The Sawtooth Wilderness is a pure habitat. Practise responsible travel by following the

"Leave No Trace" guidelines. Pack out all of your waste to reduce your environmental effect.

Respecting Wildlife

Wildlife encounters are possible. Keep a safe distance from all animals and avoid disrupting their natural behaviour.

Setting out on an Adventure

This one-day trek from Boise to the Sawtooth Wilderness is more than just a picturesque drive and walk. It is an opportunity to reconnect with nature, test your physical limits, and make memorable experiences that will enhance any Idaho adventure.

Day Trip to Coeur d'Alene from Spokane

Sparkling waterways, quaint boutiques, and a rich history make Coeur d'Alene, Idaho, an enticing day trip destination for tourists visiting Spokane, Washington. This voyage explores the core of this lakeside gem, highlighting its cultural riches, outdoor adventures, and delectable culinary scene.

A Scenic Drive and Historic Heartbeat

The drive from Spokane to Coeur d'Alene is a scenic introduction. Rolling hills emerge before you, ending in the breathtaking view of Lake Coeur d'Alene. When you arrive in downtown Coeur d'Alene, you are greeted warmly. Sherman Avenue, the dynamic hub, is home to a great selection of locally owned stores selling homemade gifts and regional delights.

Museum of North Idaho

For history buffs, the Museum of North Idaho provides a fascinating journey through time. The museum is housed in a beautifully renovated 1908 Carnegie library building and showcases the region's rich tapestry. Interactive exhibits explore the Coeur d'Alene Tribe's past, the fortitude of early settlers, and the silver mining boom that moulded the region's character. Admire beautiful beadwork and traditional attire, which reflect the indigenous population's artistic past.

Enjoying Local Flavour with a Waterfront View

After exploring history, a delicious food adventure awaits. There are numerous restaurants along the coastline, each offering a taste of the region. Choose a table on a sunny patio that overlooks the lake. Imagine the calm lapping of waves on the shore while you eat freshly caught trout and Idaho-grown vegetables. Pair this beautiful dish with a drink of local huckleberry lemonade, a delightful beverage that embodies the flavour of the region.

Explore the Sparkling Waters

No trip to Coeur d'Alene is complete without seeing the beauty of Lake Coeur d'Alene firsthand. There are numerous options available to water aficionados. Rent a kayak for a relaxing cruise around the crystal-clear sea and magnificent scenery. Observe cheerful otters frolicking close and bald eagles soaring overhead, demonstrating the region's abundance of wildlife. For a more thrilling activity, try stand-up paddleboarding or a picturesque boat cruise that provides educational commentary on the lake's history and hidden coves.

A Farewell Bathed in Sunset Splendor

Take a leisurely stroll down Coeur d'Alene's famed boardwalk as the sun sets below the horizon, painting the sky in bright hues. Street entertainers entertain the masses, and multicoloured lights illuminate the landscape, creating a festive mood. Enjoy a scoop of huckleberry ice cream as a delicious way to end your day trip journey.

Coeur d'Alene's allure extends beyond a simple day vacation. This lakeside treasure promises an amazing experience with its rich history and enchanting natural beauty, as well as its welcoming community and excellent cuisine. As you return to Spokane, your memories of Coeur d'Alene will definitely remain, enticing you back for more exploration in the future.

Snake River Canyon from Twin Falls

The Snake River Canyon, a massive gash carved into the earth by a relentless river, exemplifies nature's raw force. My recent expedition of this geological marvel, which began in the beautiful city of Twin Falls, presented a landscape of breathtaking views, secret waterfalls, and thrilling adventures.

Shoshone Falls

My voyage began at the breathtaking Shoshone Falls, also known as the "Niagara of the West." Towering 212 feet, the cascading water generates a thunderous boom and a captivating rainbow that appears to invite tourists further into the canyon's embrace. Observation decks provide breathtaking views, allowing you to appreciate the overwhelming power and beauty of this natural wonder. Informative exhibits explain the history and geological significance of the falls, helping you better appreciate this amazing scene.

Canyon Rim Trail

The Canyon Rim Trail is a must-do if you want to get a panoramic view. This paved route sweeps gracefully along the canyon's edge, providing stunning views at each turn. The multi-hued rocks, painted in red, orange, and brown, provide a stunning background to the Snake River, a brilliant turquoise ribbon that flows far below. Keep a watch out for bighorn sheep magnificently perched on the rocky outcrops, which lend a touch of nature to this already breathtaking picture. Interpretive signage explains the canyon's geological history, illustrating how millions of years of erosion shaped this breathtaking natural beauty.

Unveiling Hidden Gems

The Snake River Canyon contains gems that lie beyond the well-trodden trails. Adventurers can go on a daring rappel down the canyon walls to experience the river's raw force from a different perspective. Guided tours assure safety and improve the enjoyment of this thrilling pastime.

Hidden waterfalls in the canyon include Auger Falls and Pillar Falls, which can be reached by difficult but rewarding walks. Kayak aficionados can take an incredible adventure through the canyon's twists and turns, paddling beneath towering cliffs and witnessing the Snake River's strength firsthand.

Photography Tips

For those wanting to immortalise the canyon's grandeur, consider these photographic tips:

Wide-Angle Lens

Capture the canyon's vastness in a single frame.

Embrace Light and Darkness

Early mornings and nights provide the most dramatic lighting for stunning photographs.

Hold Steady your Shot

Use a tripod to get sharp shots, especially in windy circumstances.

Investigate the Specifics

Zoom in on intricate rock formations, vivid wildflowers, and the Snake River's turquoise ribbon to create a diverse visual tale.

Respectful Exploration

The Snake River Canyon deserves our full regard. Here are some recommendations for a sustainable and responsible visit:

Stay on the Prescribed Trails

This reduces erosion while protecting the canyon's flora and animals.

Leave no Trace

Pack out all of your garbage and leave the environment immaculate.

Respect Wildlife

Observe animals from a distance and avoid harming their natural habitat.

Maintain Enough Hydration

Bring plenty of water, especially in the summer, to keep yourself hydrated in the hot weather.

Twin Falls

After discovering the canyon's attractions, relax in the beautiful city of Twin Falls. Take a trip across the renowned Perrine Bridge, cool down in the lovely waters of Shoshone Falls Park, or relax in the Visitor Center's natural spring pool. Several restaurants with beautiful views serve delectable meals, allowing you to share your adventures over a gratifying post-canyon exploring feast.

A trip to the Snake River Canyon from Twin Falls guarantees an amazing adventure, whether you are looking for spectacular views, thrilling activities, or a peek into the canyon's hidden secrets. So bring your spirit of adventure, respect for the environment, and a camera to record the canyon's breathtaking beauty.

Silver City Ghost Town from Boise

Silver City, a charming ghost town whispering stories of bygone times, is nestled in the rugged grandeur of Owyhee County, Idaho. This engaging day excursion from Boise takes you on a tour through Idaho's vivid mining history, bringing the past to life through vestiges of a once bustling village.

A Scenic Journey to Owyhee County

The adventure begins with a picturesque drive west from Boise on Interstate 84. Lush farmland gradually changes into rolling hills interrupted by sagebrush and juniper, creating a picture of

Idaho's various landscapes. Approximately 60 miles into the drive, Owyhee County emerges, a place rich in mining heritage. Ghost towns and abandoned mining camps act as quiet sentinels for those seeking fortune.

Exploring Local Lore at the Owyhee County Historical Museum

A visit to the Owyhee County Historical Museum in Marsing provides an important introduction to the Silver City story. Faded images, mining equipment, and historical records provide a vivid picture of the silver rush that drew prospectors to this distant corner of the state. This interactive experience connects visitors to the goals and struggles of those who formed Silver City's history.

Unveiling Silver City

Following a winding road, we arrive in Silver City, where the dusty plains and worn architecture serve as a harsh yet compelling witness to the town's history. As we walk down the dead town's main street, our imaginations take flight, conjuring up images of crowded saloons, general stores loaded with supplies, and miners discussing their findings for the day. The ruins of the Owyhee Hotel, a once-grand facility that accommodated tired travellers, serve as a mute witness to the town's transformation. The Assay Office, where the value of precious metals was established, conjures up images of nervous miners anticipating their prospective windfalls.

Silver City Cemetery

A heartbreaking visit to Silver City Cemetery illustrates the town's itinerant inhabitants. Weathered headstones with faded inscriptions reveal details about the lives lost during this frontier chapter. Each name conveys a narrative, an ambition of making it big in the silver mines. The solemn setting emphasises the human element of the mining boom and its long-term impact.

From Boomtown to Ghost Town

Silver City's heyday began in the 1860s with the discovery of a large silver deposit. Within a decade, the community grew to over 2,500 residents. Saloons, gambling halls, and general stores thrived to accommodate the inflow of prospectors. However, like other mining towns, prosperity was temporary. By the early twentieth century, the silver deposits had depleted, resulting in a slow decline and the town's final abandonment.

The Silver City Historical Society's Endeavours

Despite its desolate status, Silver City thrives as a living museum, a tribute to Idaho's rich mining history. The Silver City Historical Society's tireless efforts play an important part in preserving the town's heritage. Through rigorous restoration work, they provide visitors with a glimpse of the town's past liveliness. Furthermore, the Society arranges historical events throughout the year, reviving Silver City's buried stories and ensuring its position in Idaho's historical tapestry.

A Day Trip Full with History

As we leave Silver City in the dying light, the spirit of the Wild West lingers. This day excursion goes beyond a simple sightseeing adventure, providing a compelling voyage back in time. We return to Boise with a new respect for Idaho's history, eternally enriched by the echoes of the past that still ring behind the walls of Silver City.

Chapter 7: Conclusion

Safety Tips for Tourists

Idaho's breathtaking mountains, pure lakes, and compelling wild places entice adventurers from all over the world. While the joy of exploration is evident, putting safety first is critical for a successful and enriching adventure. This guide provides you with crucial ideas for navigating Idaho's different landscapes and having a worry-free journey.

Respecting Mother Nature's Power
Idaho's diversified landscape features significant weather variations. Here's how to prepare for the elements and have a comfortable exploration:

Layered Clothing

Pack versatile clothes that can be easily layered. Choose moisture-wicking base layers, insulating midlayers, and a waterproof outer garment. Remember to pack a hat and sunglasses for sun protection, as well as strong hiking boots for uneven terrain.

Hydration is Essential

Dehydration can occur quickly, particularly during summer excursions or intense activity. Carry a reusable water bottle and drink often throughout the day. Choose water or electrolyte-replenishing beverages over sugary ones.

Sun Safety

Idaho's high elevation amplifies the sun's rays. Use a broad-spectrum sunscreen liberally and reapply every two hours, especially after swimming or sweating.

Winter Preparedness

Pack warm garments and insulated boots with good traction for winter trips. On ice terrain, consider employing traction aids such as microspikes or crampons. Before heading into snowy places, be aware of the potential for avalanches and examine weather forecasts.

Fire Safety

Idaho experiences dry summers, which raises the risk of wildfires. Always follow campfire limits and extinguish any flames correctly. Familiarise yourself with fire safety measures to reduce the possibility of an accidental wildfire.

Wildlife Encounters

Idaho is home to a diverse range of animals, from stately elk to playful otters. Understanding correct etiquette minimises disruption to these animals while also ensuring your safety:

Bear Awareness

Black bears and grizzly bears live in specific areas of Idaho. Carrying bear spray and learning good application techniques is critical. Food and toiletries should be stored in bear-proof containers or designated lockers at campgrounds. Make noise when hiking, especially in regions with little visibility, to alert bears to your presence.

Respecting Snake Territory

Rattlesnakes and other dangerous snakes live in several locations of Idaho. Stay cautious on the paths, wear strong boots, and avoid putting your hands or feet where you can not see. If you come across a snake, simply back away and give it space.

Leave No Trace

Reduce your influence on wildlife by properly disposing of food scraps and rubbish. Avoid leaving food unattended since it can attract unwanted animals and alter natural behaviour.

Essential Tips for Outdoor Adventure

Idaho's extensive wilderness provides a playground for adventure lovers. Here are some important safety guidelines for a successful and fun adventure:

Inform Others

Before embarking on a hike or backcountry expedition, notify a friend, family member, or park ranger of your intended route and expected return time. This enables for quicker assistance in the event of an emergency.

Plan your Route

Before setting out on your chosen trail, do some research to learn about its difficulty level, duration, and potential risks. Always have a map and compass, and consider downloading offline maps to your phone for backup.

Be Weather Aware

Check the weather forecast before going out, and be prepared for unexpected changes. Avoid travelling into hazardous weather conditions that could jeopardise your safety.

Know Your Limits

Do not push yourself beyond your physical limits. Choose trails based on your fitness level and experience. Take regular pauses and do not be afraid to turn back if you become exhausted or lost.

Carry Essentials

Pack a backpack with first-aid supplies, an emergency whistle, a torch or flashlight with spare batteries, and a waterproof poncho or rain jacket. Consider carrying a personal locating beacon (PLB) in remote places with minimal cell connectivity.

Safety in the City

While exploring Idaho's lovely communities and vibrant cities, keep these safety guidelines in mind:

Street Smart

As in any metropolis, remain vigilant and mindful of your surroundings. Trust your intuition and avoid poorly lighted or remote roadways at night.

Parking Smartly

Choose well-lit parking locations, especially if you are leaving your car overnight. Avoid leaving valuables in plain sight inside your vehicle.

Be Firearm Aware

Open carry legislation exists in Idaho. If you are inexperienced with firearms, be aware of this legislation and remain calm if you see someone openly carrying a firearm.

Useful Phrases for Travelers

As a valued visitor to Idaho, also known as the "Gem State," effective communication can significantly enhance your experience. This guide equips you with essential phrases to navigate various situations during your trip, fostering a sense of connection with the welcoming Idahoan community.

Greetings and Establishing Rapport

• Formal: "Good morning/afternoon/evening!" A courteous greeting appropriate for any interaction.

• Informal: "Hi there!" or "Hello!" Suitable for casual settings.

- Initiating Conversation: "How are you today?" followed by "I'm doing well, thank you. How are you?" demonstrates genuine interest.

- Introductions: "Nice to meet you!" establishes a friendly connection when encountering someone for the first time.

Seeking Assistance and Expressing Gratitude

- Gaining Attention: "Excuse me" politely initiates interaction when requesting assistance.

- Asking for Directions: "Can you please point me in the direction of...?" followed by the specific location.

- Confirmation: "Is this the way to...?" politely verifies you're on the correct path.

- Appreciation: "Thank you" expresses gratitude in any situation. "Thank you very much" emphasises your appreciation.

- Responding to Thanks: "You're welcome" is a standard response.

Phrases for Transactions and Inquiries

- Prices: "How much does this cost?" inquires about the price of an item.

- Payment Methods: "Do you accept credit cards?" confirms accepted payment options.

- Additional Needs: "May I please have a bag for this?" requests a shopping bag for your purchase.

- Understanding Local Terms: Be prepared to encounter terms like "huckleberry" (a delicious wild berry), "crick" (a small stream), or "rig" (a large SUV/truck).

Dining Etiquette and Requests

- Complimenting Cuisine: "This is delicious!" expresses your appreciation for the food.

- Ordering: "I would like to order the..." followed by your chosen dish.

- Settling the Bill: "May I please have the check?" politely requests your bill after your meal.

- Dietary Restrictions: "Do you have vegetarian/vegan options available?" inquires about catering to dietary needs.

Engaging in Meaningful Conversation

- Conversation Starters: "The weather is beautiful today, isn't it?" or "I'm enjoying my visit to Idaho. The scenery is breathtaking!" can spark friendly conversation.

- Seeking Recommendations: "What are some must-see attractions in this area?" demonstrates your interest in local insights.

- Sharing Background: "I'm visiting from..." allows for cultural exchange.

Optional but Helpful: Basic Spanish Phrases

While English is the primary language, a significant portion of Idaho's population speaks Spanish. Learning a few basic phrases can be advantageous:

• Hola! (Hello!)

• Gracias. (Thank you.)

• No hablo mucho español. (I don't speak much Spanish.)

• ¿Habla usted inglés? (Do you speak English?)

Beyond Words: Importance of Nonverbal Communication

Effective communication extends beyond spoken language. Maintaining eye contact, offering a friendly smile, and using polite gestures like nodding can significantly enhance your interactions with Idahoans.

Embrace the Local Lingo: Immerse Yourself in the Culture

These phrases provide a foundation, but the most enriching way to learn the local language is through everyday interactions. Strike up conversations with shopkeepers, greet locals with a courteous "good morning," and don't be afraid to ask questions. Embrace the opportunity to connect with the welcoming spirit of Idaho and create lasting memories in the Gem State.

Printed in Great Britain
by Amazon